BLACK
PEARLS
JOURNAL

ALSO BY ERIC V. COPAGE

Black Pearls for Parents

Black Pearls

*Kwanzaa: An African-American Celebration
of Culture and Cooking*

BLACK PEARLS JOURNAL

Eric V. Copage

William Morrow and Company, Inc.
New York

It is the policy of William Morrow and Company, Inc., and its
imprints and affiliates, recognizing the importance of preserving
what has been written, to print the books we publish on acid-
free paper, and we exert our best efforts to that end.

LIBRARY OF CONGRESS CATALOGING-IN-PUBLICATION DATA
Copage, Eric V.
Black pearls journal / Eric V. Copage.
p.   cm.
Includes index.
ISBN 0-688-13967-1
1. Afro-Americans—Life skills guides. I. Title.
E185.86.C5882   1995
305.896'073—dc20
94-3417
CIP

Printed in the United States of America

First Edition

1 2 3 4 5 6 7 8 9 10

BOOK DESIGN BY RICHARD ORIOLO

To the writer /reader of this journal

INTRODUCTION

To begin a journal is to embark upon a journey. Sometimes that journey is into the past—a childhood experience, a pivotal life event, a tender moment with a spouse. Sometimes that journey is into the future—battle plans for upcoming projects, planning a child's education, or simply a movie not to be missed. And sometimes the journal itself is a vehicle for a journey: We transport ourselves into the new self-understanding by putting things into perspective, blowing off steam, cheering ourselves up, articulating dreams, and giving ourselves encouragement within the covers of our book. In our writings we can explore what nurtures us and what gives us pleasure or satisfaction.

But a journal needn't necessarily be a tunnel to the past, a freeway to the future, or a bridge to greater self-understanding. A journal can also simply be a road map of the day's events, a notation of birthdays, anniversaries, of people met or to meet, things to do and things done.

A journal can be all of the above at once or at different times, as dictated by our whim and want. When embarking upon a journal, there is no need to predetermine our destination.

It's also important to remember that when keeping a journal we needn't create a prize-winning book. Writing can be a great outlet for our stress and a way to express thoughts and feelings we find difficult to share. When critically acclaimed novelist Gloria Naylor was twelve, her mother gave her a dairy, which began a habit of keeping notebooks and journals. Naylor credits these writings with allowing her to get her "life in order."

Whether Naylor knew it then or not, journal writing, which after all is a kind of autobiography, has a long tradition among African Americans. Slave narratives, memoirs, and autobiographies dot our literary landscape, bearing witness to our spiritual strength, our humanity, and our complexity. These writings preserve stories that would have been lost as generations grew old and died.

In short, keeping a journal, whether it is to preserve the iridescent scrim of feeling and thought or to catalog mundane things and events, makes each and every one of us a custodian of our people, by bearing witness to the world around us and, more important, documenting our impressions of our own lives. The observations of any single individual may seem insignificant compared to the great tumult of life around us. But, to quote former slave Lucy Delaney's remark in the preface to her 1891 narrative, "Although we are each but atoms, it must be remembered that we assist in making the grand total of human history." We must remember that black men and women have never hesitated to put pen to paper to preserve their powerful stories, to plan their future, and to record the facts of their existence. Let us now continue that tradition, pick up our pen, and bear witness with whatever type of entry we are moved to record.

BLACK
PEARLS
JOURNAL

FAITH

I've had so many downs that I knew the law of averages
would be in my favor one day.
—*Doug Williams*

On this day, I

_____ *date*

PLANNING

I don't like short-term solutions; they can come back
and bite you in the behind later.

—*Caroline R. Jones*

 *On this day, I*

date _____

HERITAGE

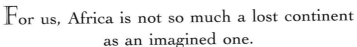

For us, Africa is not so much a lost continent
as an imagined one.

—*Jack E. White*

On this day, I

_____ *date*

ASSERTIVENESS

I made speech my birthright ... talking back became
for me a rite of initiation.

—*bell hooks*

On this day, I

date _____

RENEWAL

When things got bad, I'd just sing "Ave Maria," which is one of my favorite songs from childhood . . . it was my salvation. It gave me a reason to believe that things would change.

—*Aaron Neville*

 On this day, I

_____*date*

CHILDHOOD

... they'll probably talk about my hard childhood and never
understand that all the while I was quite happy.

—*Nikki Giovanni*

On this day, I

*date*_____

SELF-RELIANCE

Self-help is the best help.

—*Aesop, from "Hercules and the Wagoner"*

On this day, I

date

Harmony

If we do not work at releasing the inharmonious thoughts and
attitudes that grow deep within, there is nothing that
mere physical release can do for us.

—Juliette McGinnis, stress management therapist

On this day, I

date _____

BEGINNING

The first thing I typed was my name. I wanted to see how it looked in print. Then I began to type my poems.

—*August Wilson*

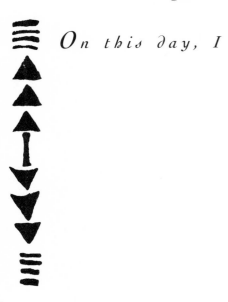

On this day, I

_____ *date*

RELAXATION

I couldn't figure out why I was tired ... why all these people
kept saying they had a hard time catching up with me and,
eventually, stopped trying.

—*Ntozake Shange*

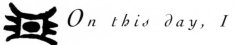 *On this day, I*

*date*_____

DIETING/LOVE

When I fell in love, I'd lose weight and then when the relationship failed, I'd gain it back. Food and heartache are intertwined within me.

—*Luther Vandross*

 *On this day, I*

_____ *date*

OPTIMISM

I want to see how life can triumph.

—*Romare Bearden*

On this day, I

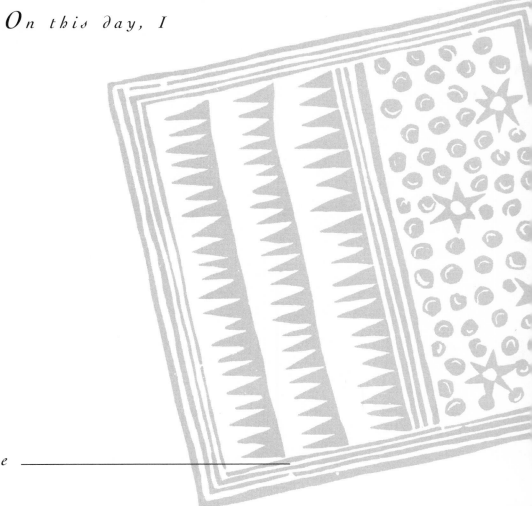

date _____

INDEPENDENCE

Being your own man does not mean taking
advantage of anyone else.

—*Flip Wilson*

 On this day, I

_____ *date*

PURPOSE

The dog has four feet, but he does not walk them in four roads.

—Haitian proverb

 On this day, I

date _____

COLLECTIVE RESPONSIBILITY

We rarely goes down by ourse'fs.

—*John Jasper*

On this day, I

_____ *date*

COURAGE

The higher the monkey climbs, the more it is exposed to danger.
—*Belizean proverb*

On this day, I

date _____

GOD

....

People see God every day; they just don't recognize Him.
—*Pearl Bailey*

On this day, I

_____ ∂ a t e

SELF-DETERMINATION

The adults in my life told me I could do anything if I was
determined and resourceful. . . . I was expected to be ambitious
because there was an intrinsic pleasure in excelling, not
because I had to prove anything to whites.

—*Eric V. Copage*

On this day, I

date _____

SPACE

There are periods when I am the most attentive and thoughtful lover in the world, and periods, too, when I am just unavailable. . . . When I "surface" again, I try to apply the poultices and patch up the holes I've left in relationships around me.

—*Toni Cade Bambara*

 On this day, I

_____ *date*

BEAUTY

When I found I had crossed dat *line*, I looked at my hands to
see if I was de same pusson. There was such a glory ober ebery
ting; de sun came like gold through de trees, and ober
de fields, and I felt like I was in Heaben.

—*Harriet Tubman*

On this day, I

date _____

MISTAKES

Every man got a right to his own mistakes.
Ain't no man that ain't made any.

—*Joe Louis*

On this day, I

_____ *date*

SELF-IMAGE

I was always told I was the ugliest. That I was the dumbest. I was the blackest. That I would never be anything. My sister was much lighter than me, thin lips. I got the thick lips, the orange hair. I got all the beatings.

—*Bertha Gilkey*

On this day, I

date _____

VISION

I have the original vision, and I see the film in its finished form
before one frame is shot. When you get people dickering
with your stuff, it distorts the vision.

—*Spike Lee*

 *On this day, I*

_____ *date*

AGING/WISDOM

The man who views the world at fifty the same as he did at twenty has wasted thirty years of his life.

—*Muhammad Ali*

On this day, I

date _____

DISCOURAGEMENT

Many times during auditions, I was told that I couldn't carry a note with a bucket, and that I sure couldn't play the piano.

—*Ray Charles*

 *On this day, I*

_____ *date*

EQUALITY AT WORK

Equals make the best friends.

—Aesop, from "The Two Pots"

On this day, I

date _____

MONEY

America is a capitalist country, and I am a capitalist.

—*Alonzo Herndon*

On this day, I

_____ *date*

FAITH

Anticipate the good so that you may enjoy it.
—*Ethiopian proverb*

 *On this day, I*

date _____

JUDGING CHARACTER

You shake man han', you no shake him heart.

—*Bahamian proverb*

 *On this day, I*

_____ *date*

AGGRESSIVENESS

God gives nothing to those who keep their arms crossed.

—*African proverb*

On this day, I

date _____

COPING

Yeah, life hurts like hell, but this is how I keep going. I have a
sense of humor, I've got my brothers and sisters. I've got the
ability to make something out of nothing. I can clap
my hands and make magic.

—*Bill T. Jones*

On this day, I

_____ *date*

AFFIRMATIVE ACTION

I'm not a threatening black person to them. . . . That's probably
why I got hired. . . . But I also got hired because
I'm good. I have all the tools.

—*Branford Marsalis*

On this day, I

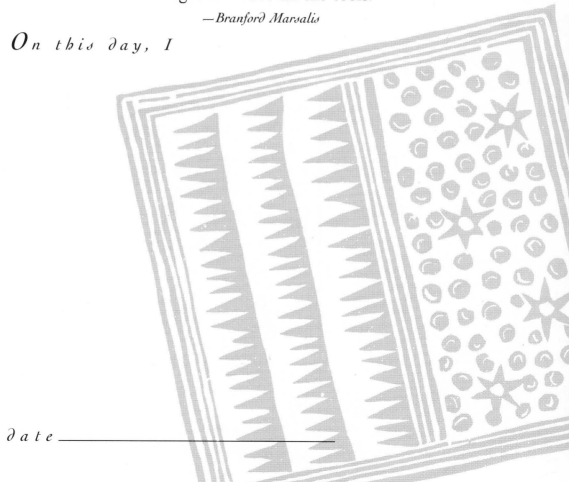

date _____

SHYNESS

I don't like making entrances unless I'm in costume,
at eight o'clock, on stage.
—Leontyne Price

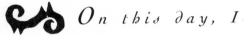 *On this day, I*

_____ *date*

TIME

We kill time; time buries us.

—*Joaquim Maria Machado de Assis*

On this day, I

date _____

DISCOURAGEMENT

We must not become discouraged.
—*Booker T. Washington*

On this day, I

_____ *date*

UNITY

Sticks in a bundle are unbreakable.

—Kenyan (Bondei) proverb

On this day, I

date _____

STRENGTH

One thing they cannot prohibit—

The strong men . . . coming on

The strong men gittin' stronger.

Strong men . . .

Stronger . . .

—Sterling Brown

On this day, I

_____ *date*

STEREOTYPES

One of the sad commentaries on the way women are viewed in our society is that we have to fit one category. I have never felt that I had to be in one category.

—*Faye Wattleton*

On this day, I

date _____

LONELINESS

There was no loneliness in the living room. So it was a good part, and maybe the best part, of the house.

—*June Jordan*

On this day, I

_____ *date*

FREEDOM

We have dared to be free; let us dare to be so by
ourselves and for ourselves.

—*Jean-Jacques Dessalines, Proclamation, January 1, 1804*

On this day, I

date _____

GENEROSITY

Before you marry keep both eyes open; after marriage shut one.

—Jamaican proverb

On this day, I

_____ *date*

ADAPTABILITY

What most successful blacks learn is that most everything can, in fact, be learned — how to talk, how to dress, how to groom an image for success. The important thing is to recognize what is not known — and then learn it.

— *Audrey Edwards and Craig K. Polite, from* Children of the Dream

On this day, I

date _____

FORETHOUGHT

Look before you leap.
—Aesop, from "The Fox and the Goats"

On this day, I

_____ *date*

PEACE

....

I hope never to be at peace. I hope to make my life manageable,
and I think it's fairly manageable now. But, oh, I would
never accept peace. That seems death.

—*Jamaica Kincaid*

On this day, I

date _____

LOVE

Love without esteem cannot go far or reach high.
It is an angel with only one wing.

—*Alexandre Dumas, fils*

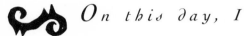 *On this day, I*

_____ *date*

SELF-HELP

"Self-help" isn't enough in a milieu of institutionalized racism.

—*Carl T. Rowan*

On this day, I

date _____

MAKING DEALS

Women don't get hung up, making deals the way men do.
—*Shirley Chisholm*

On this day, I

_____ *date*

POSITIVE THINKING

To be a great champion you must believe you are the best.
If you're not, pretend you are.

—*Muhammad Ali*

On this day, I

date _____

CONFUSION

A man is sometimes lost in the dust of his own raising.
—*David Ruggles*

On this day, I

_____ *date*

MONEY

Let the Afro-American depend on no party, but on himself for his salvation. Let him continue to education, to character, and above all, to put money in his purse. When he has money, and plenty of it, parties and races will become his servants.

—*Ida B. Wells*

 *On this day, I*

date _____

PRIDE

You can't just fight for the money because if you do, after the
first round you can think you don't need to take all the
punishment. ...You fight for the belt plus the pride.

—*Evander Holyfield*

On this day, I

date

QUIET

I love to walk on the Sabbath, for all is so peaceful, the noise and labor of everyday life has ceased; and in perfect silence we can commune with nature and with Nature's God.

—*Charlotte L. Forten*

On this day, I

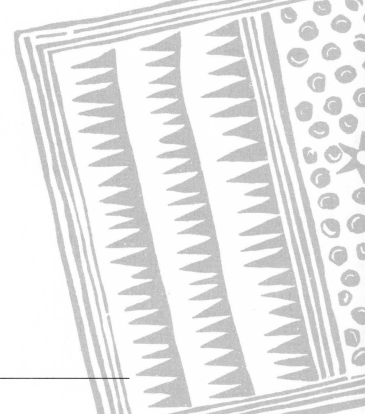

date _____

ROLE MODELS

I could see that my significance as an individual was small. . . . I had become, whether I liked it or not, a symbol, representing my people. . . . I could not run away from this situation.

—*Marian Anderson*

On this day, I

_____ *date*

CONFLICT

I glory in conflict, that I may hereafter exult in victory.

—*Frederick Douglass*

 On this day, I

date _____

RESEARCH

May God preserve us from "If I had known"!

—*Hausa proverb*

On this day, I

_____ *date*

SATISFACTION

I rewrite all the way to the printer. I'm never satisfied.
—*Toni Morrison*

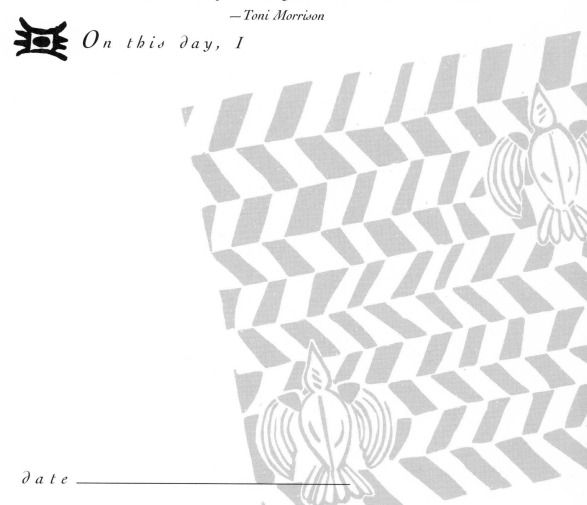

On this day, I

date _____

HELPING OTHERS

A sure way for one to lift himself up is by
helping to lift someone else.

—*Booker T. Washington*

On this day, I

_____ *date*

COLLECTIVE WORK/ COLLECTIVE RESPONSIBILITY

If farmers do not cultivate their fields, the people in
the town will die of hunger.

—*Guinean proverb*

On this day, I

date _____

CONTROL/DIRECTION

To me, Jesus was a phenomenal figure. . . . He was a
revolutionary, but He knew how to conserve His energy.

—*Wesley Snipes*

On this day, I

_____ *date*

DIPLOMACY

Maybe the worst somebody would ever say of me was: He was fairly undiplomatic in the way he tried to get things done. But at least he tried to get things done.

—*Bryant Gumbel*

On this day, I

date _____

COURAGE

Courage may be the most important of all virtues, because without it one cannot practice any other virtue with consistency.

—*Maya Angelou*

On this day, I

_____ *date*

PURPOSE

I don't know the key to success, but the key to failure
is trying to please everybody.

—*Bill Cosby*

 *On this day, I*

date _____

SACRIFICE

Becoming a world-class figure skater meant long hours of practice while sometimes tolerating painful injuries. It meant being totally exhausted sometimes, and not being able to do all the things I wanted to do when I wanted to do them.

—*Debi Thomas*

On this day, I

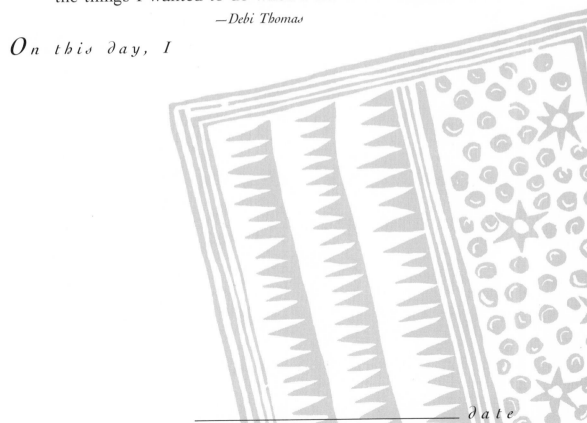

_____ *date*

FOCUSING

When I leave the ballpark, I leave everything there. When I hit the driveway, I become a husband and father.

—*Bo Jackson*

On this day, I

date _____

INDIVIDUAL RESPONSIBILITY

It is impossible to raise and educate a race in the mass. All revolutions and improvements must start with individuals.

—*John W. E. Bowen*

On this day, I

_____ *date*

PERSEVERANCE

I'm inspired when I walk down the street and still see people trying. A lot of them look as if they're on their last leg, but they're still getting up somehow.

—*Faith Ringgold*

On this day, I

date _____

FIRST STEPS

I knew someone had to take the first step and I made
up my mind not to move.
—*Rosa Parks*

On this day, I

_____ date

EXCELLENCE

Strive to make something of yourselves; then
strive to make the most of yourselves.

—*Alexander Crummell*

 On this day, I

date _____

POWER

There does not have to be powerlessness.
The power is within ourselves.
—*Faye Wattleton*

On this day, I

_____ *date*

PRIDE

The only excuse for pride in individuals or races is the fact of their own achievements.

—*Frederick Douglass*

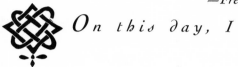 *On this day, I*

date _____

EDUCATION

The masses must move, but it must be
the classes that move them.
—*William Saunders Scarborough*

On this day, I

_____ *date*

CHANGE

Every small, positive change we can make in ourselves
repays us in confidence in the future.

—*Alice Walker*

On this day, I

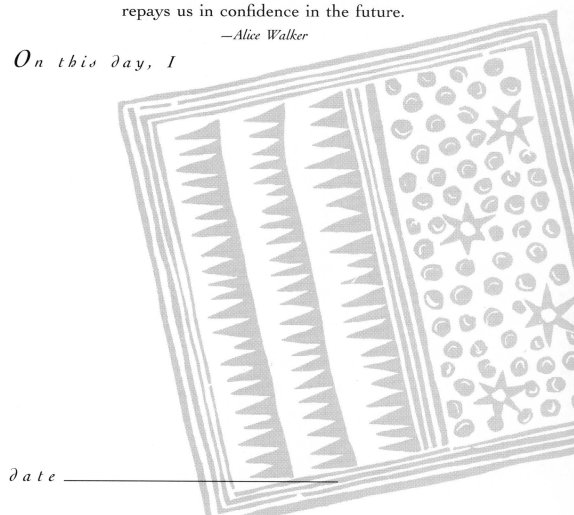

date _____

SUCCESS

In some sense, the black professional's problem is that each of us
who succeeds in the white world feels we've succeeded at
the expense of our brothers.

—*Kenneth McClane*

On this day, I

_____ *date*

PRIVACY

Black people don't have any privacy.

—Anonymous, heard in Harlem

On this day, I

date _____

EXPERIMENTATION

People have to have permission to write, and they have to be given the space to breathe and stumble. They have to be given time to develop and to reveal what they can do.

—*Toni Cade Bambara*

On this day, I

_____ *date*

OPTIMISM

What seems to be a great loss or punishment often turns out to be a blessing. I know, through my own experience, that God never closes one door without opening another.

—*Yolande D. Herron*

On this day, I

*date*_____

DEPENDENCY

The greatest thing I ever was able to do was give a welfare
check back. I brought it back . . . and said, "Here.
I don't need this anymore."

— *Whoopi Goldberg*

On this day, I

_____ *date*

ANGER

When you clench your fist, no one can put anything in your
hand, nor can your hand pick up anything.

—*Alex Haley, from* Roots

On this day, I

date _____

PERSEVERANCE

By trying often, the monkey learns to jump from the tree.
—*Cameroon proverb*

On this day, I

_____ *date*

PREJUDICE

Terms like "prejudice" and "racism" often miss the full scope of racial devaluation in our society, implying as they do that racial devaluation comes primarily from the strongly prejudiced, not from "good people."

—*Claude M. Steele*

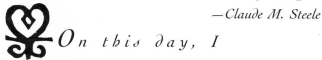*On this day, I*

*date*_____

ETERNITY

It is only what is written upon the soul of man that will
survive the wreck of time.

—*Francis Grimké*

On this day, I

_____ *date*

SELF-RELIANCE

Everyone is more or less the master of his own fate.

—Aesop, from "The Traveler and Fortune"

On this day, I

date _____

EMOTIONS

Our feelings are our most genuine paths to knowledge. They are chaotic, sometimes painful, sometimes contradictory, but they come from deep within us. And we must key into those feelings. . . . This is how new visions begin.

—*Audre Lorde*

On this day, I

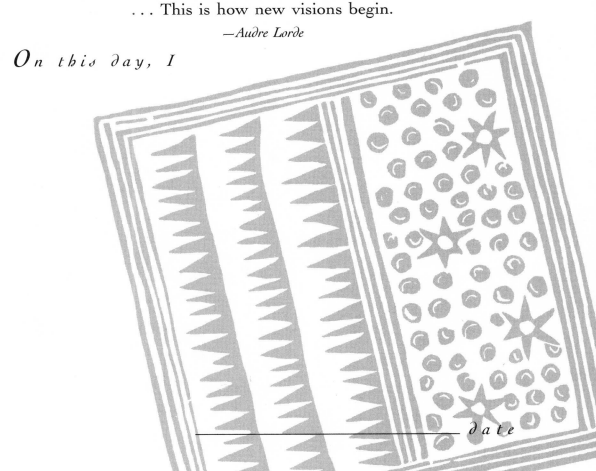

_____ *date*

FEAR

You got people out there with this scar on their brains, and they will carry that scar to their graves. The mark of fear is not easily removed.

—*Ernest J. Gaines, from* The Autobiography of Miss Jane Pittman

On this day, I

date _____

TRUST

I am not afraid to trust my sisters—not I.

—*Angelina Grimké*

On this day, I

_____ *date*

WHITE PEOPLE

If I stepped back and thought about it, I wouldn't be able to do
what I do and deal with the type of people I deal with.
Because I deal with a lot of white people.

—*Maurice Starr*

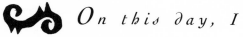 *On this day, I*

SELF-DETERMINATION

The Negro was invented in America.

—*John Oliver Killens*

On this day, I

_____ *date*

DIPLOMACY

You worry too much about what goes into your mouth and
not enough about what comes out of it.

—*Leah Chase*

On this day, I

date _____

IMPEDIMENTS

I tell my students there is such a thing as "writer's block," and
they should respect it. It's blocked because it ought to be
blocked, because you haven't got it right now.

— *Toni Morrison*

On this day, I

———————————————————— *date*

IMAGINATION

Dream big dreams! Others may deprive you of your material wealth and cheat you in a thousand ways, but no man can deprive you of the control and use of your imagination.

—*Jesse Jackson*

 On this day, I

date _____

SAVING MONEY

Save money and money will save you.

—*Jamaican proverb*

On this day, I

_____ *date*

WELL-BEING

Hair and teeth—a man got those two things, he's got it all.
—*James Brown*

On this day, I

*date*_____

PACING

There's no need to hurry, yet no time to lose.

—*Bessie Copage*

On this day, I

_____ *date*

BEING BLACK

I've always been proud to be black. But proud and obsessive are different things.

—*Jacob Lamar*

On this day, I

date _____

CREATIVITY

Do a common thing in an uncommon way.
—*Booker T. Washington*

On this day, I

_____ *date*

CONSIDERATION

Our society allows people to be absolutely neurotic and totally
out of touch with their feelings and everyone else's feelings,
and yet be very respectable.

—*Ntozake Shange*

On this day, I

date _____

MIND POWER

It is the mind that makes the body.
—*Sojourner Truth*

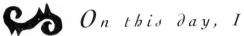 *On this day, I*

_____ *date*

STRUGGLE

You cannot fight by being on the outside complaining and whining. You have to get on the inside to be able to assess their strengths and weaknesses and then move in.

—*Shirley Chisholm*

On this day, I

date _____

LOVE

I have cared for more than six hundred addicted babies since we opened the center. . . . They love you to tell them how great they are, how good they are. Somehow, even at a young age, they understand that.

—*Clara "Mother" Hale*

On this day, I

_____ *date*

BUILDING

Our children may learn about heroes of the past. Our task is to make ourselves architects of the future.

—Jomo Kenyatta

On this day, I

date_____

FAILURE

I don't believe in failure. It is not failure if
you enjoyed the process.
—*Oprah Winfrey*

 On this day, I

_____ *date*

READING

It often requires more courage to read some books
than it does to fight a battle.

—*Sutton E. Griggs*

On this day, I

date _____

COMMUNICATION

We're living in an age when people need to talk.
They don't communicate.

—*Queen Latifah*

On this day, I

—————————————————— *date*

PRIVATE TIME

We shouldn't depend on the outside world for our happiness;
we should have our private world where we go for some peace.
So we must be careful about how we build our private worlds.

—*J. California Cooper*

On this day, I

date _____

TIMING

The best time to do a thing is when it can be done.

—*William Pickens*

On this day, I

_____ *date*

LOVE

I've heard some of the young people laugh about slave love, but
they should envy the love which kept mother and father so
close together in life, and even held them in death.

—Alonzo Haywood, former enslaved African-American

On this day, I

date _____

PURPOSE

Little by little the bird makes its nest.
—*Haitian proverb*

On this day, I

_____ *date*

SELF-RESPECT

If you respect yourself, it's easier to respect other people.

—*John Singleton*

On this day, I

date _____

COMPULSIVENESS

When do any of us ever do enough?
—*Barbara Jordan*

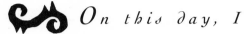 *On this day, I*

_____ *date*

SELF-DETERMINATION

Acceptance of prevailing standards often means we
have no standards of our own.

—*Jean Toomer*

On this day, I

date _____

AMBITION

I stood up in front of a speech class and said, "I plan to make my living with my oratory skills, and I'd like to be a talk show host." There was a pause, then the most incredible laughter you've ever heard in your life.

—*Arsenio Hall*

On this day, I

_____ *date*

MORTALITY

I never thought I would live to be forty. . . . I am stronger
for confronting the hard issue of breast cancer,
of mortality, dying.

—Audre Lorde

On this day, I

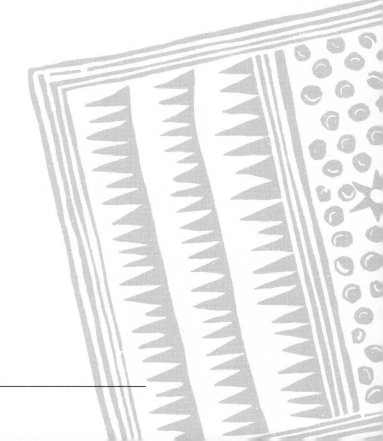

date _____

FULFILLMENT

A few years ago, I just thought about winning. When I won, I was happy and when I lost, I was unhappy. Now I am happy in my circumstances, even when I lose. That's my decision, not an excuse, because I like how I am and what I'm doing.

—*Yannick Noah*

On this day, I

_____ *date*

Contributing

I believe in helping people the best way you can; my way is through my art. But sometimes you need a splash of cold water in your face to make you see the right way to do it.

—*Arthur Mitchell*

On this day, I

date _____

BALANCE

I try to balance my life. When I'm home, I give quality time. . . .
I'm happy I've achieved what I have without losing my head.
—*Patti LaBelle*

On this day, I

_____ *date*

ALIENATION

Half the time I feel like I'm on the outside of the world
peeping in through a knot-hole in the fence.

—*Richard Wright, from* Native Son

On this day, I

date _____

MULTIFACETEDNESS

I knew that if a music career wasn't going to happen, I could do
other things to make my contribution—medicine was one,
and I was also interested in law.

—*Barbara Hendricks*

On this day, I

_____ *date*

PREJUDICE

I believe in recognizing every human being as a human being—
neither white, black, brown, or red.

—*Malcolm X*

 *On this day, I*

date _____

POTENTIAL

A mind is a terrible thing to waste.
—*The United Negro College Fund*

On this day, I

_____ *date*

STRUGGLE

If murderers come to kill you, you do not say, "I cannot oppose
the next stab wound because my life is already forfeit."
No—you fight for your life!

—*Hermon George, Jr.*

On this day, I

date _____

SUCCESS

I used to want the words "She tried" on my tombstone.
Now I want "She did it."
—*Katherine Dunham*

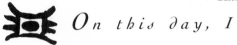 *On this day, I*

_____ *date*

RELATIONSHIPS

I know now that no other woman
can take the place of a man's mother,
and that no man can take the place
of a woman's father.

—*Quincy Jones*

On this day, I

date _____

QUESTIONING

All over the world, nobody has a God who doesn't resemble
them. Except black Americans. They can't even see they're
worshipping someone else's God, because they want
so badly to assimilate.

—*August Wilson*

On this day, I

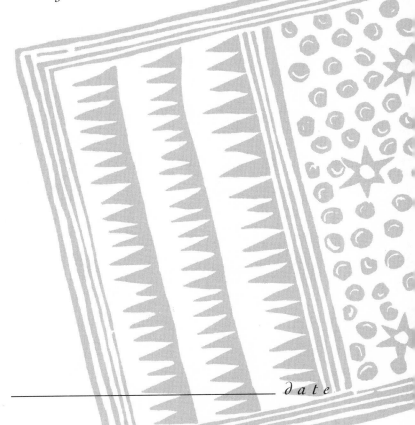

_____ *date*

SELF-CONFIDENCE

If you have no confidence in self, you are twice defeated in the
race of life. With confidence, you have won even
before you have started.

—*Marcus Garvey*

On this day, I

date _____

NETWORKING

A single bracelet does not jingle.
— *Congo proverb*

On this day, I

_____ *date*

OBSTACLES

We must use time creatively . . . and forever realize that
the time is always ripe to do right.

—*Martin Luther King, Jr.*

On this day, I

date _____

ENVY

Do not despise or hate your neighbor because he has been a
success; take care of your own case.

—*William T. Vernon*

On this day, I

_____ *date*

PREPARATION

You cannot shave a man's head in his absence.
—*Yoruba proverb*

On this day, I

date _____

SLOGANEERING

I'd rather see a cat with a processed head and a natural mind than a natural head and a processed mind.

—*H. Rap Brown*

On this day, I

_____ *date*

ANGER

Anger is an emotion that if you carry around over a long period
of time, it doesn't allow you to live.

—*John Singleton*

On this day, I

date _____

INDEPENDENCE

We had a strong relationship based on mutual respect and love. I had to go through a difficult struggle, searching for someone to replace [my teacher], someone who could say, "Never mind, this is what's important." I finally found that person in myself.

—*Barbara Hendricks*

On this day, I

_____ *date*

PROBLEMS

When it rains, the roof always drips the same way.

—Jabo proverb

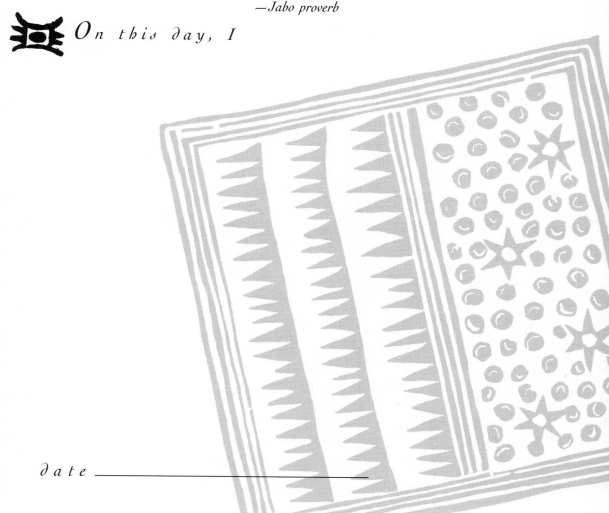

On this day, I

date _____

PLEASURE

While I can't say there was a particular moment when I attended a concert, heard a piece and was overwhelmed, music was always around, and I just sang for the pleasure of it.

—*Barbara Hendricks*

On this day, I

_____ *date*

SELF-DETERMINATION

I'd continue to teach my children what I had been taught: that they needn't see a black become president or win the Indy 500 on television before they could do it in real life.

—*Eric V. Copage*

On this day, I

date _____

AMBITION

The ladder of success is never crowded at the top.
—*Florence Griffith Joyner*

On this day, I

_____ *date*

SELF-WORTH

A man's vocation is no measure for his inner feelings nor a
guarantee of his earnest desire to live right and attain
the highest standards.

—*Jack Johnson*

On this day, I

date _____

STRESS

Excessive or prolonged stress, particularly in the form of frustration, fear or anxiety, is distress, and it leads to disease.

—*Gail C. Christopher*

 On this day, I

_____ *date*

LOSING

Losses always attend moving.
—*Charles V. Roman*

On this day, I

date _____

LOVE

To love is to make of one's heart a swinging door.
—*Howard Thurman*

On this day, I

_____ *date*

DECISIONS

I taped the application
and *ironed* it.

*—Debi Thomas, who tore up an application for the U. S. Figure Skating
Championship—then changed her mind and went on to win the title.*

On this day, I

date _____

OPENNESS

To be a great musician, you've got to be open to what's new, what's happening at the moment. You have to be able to absorb it if you're going to continue to grow and communicate.

—*Miles Davis*

On this day, I

_____ *date*

PERFECTION

No one is perfect in this imperfect world.

—Patrice Lumumba

 *On this day, I*

date _____

ACCOMMODATION

Living together is an art.
—*William Pickens*

On this day, I

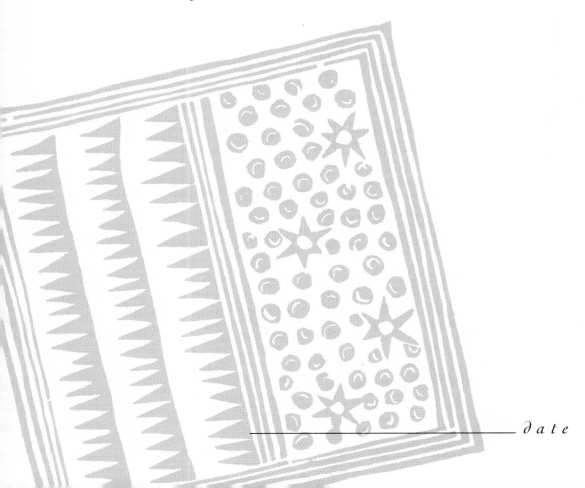

_____ date

CHANGE

To change is to be vulnerable. And to be
vulnerable is to be alive.

—*Alexis De Veaux*

 *On this day, I*

date _____

REJECTION

I have learned to take "no" as a vitamin.
—*Suzanne De Passe*

On this day, I

_____ *date*

FLEXIBILITY/
DETERMINATION

You can map out a fight plan or a life plan, but when the action starts, it may not go the way you planned, and you're down to your reflexes—which means your training.

—*Joe Frazier*

On this day, I

*date*_____

EFFICIENCY

If initiative is the ability to do the right thing, then efficiency is
the ability to do the thing right.

—*Kelly Miller*

On this day, I

_____ *date*

PLAY

It is an emergency for me to learn how to play. It is something I don't know how to do. I've never just taken time off and played.

—*Bernice Johnson Reagon*

On this day, I

date _____

AGGRESSIVENESS

I had to make my own opportunity. . . . Don't sit down and wait
for the opportunities to come; you have to get
up and make them.
—*Madame C. J. Walker*

On this day, I

_____ *date*

CREATIVITY

There is a use for almost everything.

—*George Washington Carver*

On this day, I

date _____

SEX

Blacks comprise 14% of New York State's population, but in 1991 comprised 40% of the state's AIDS cases. "AIDS in future generations may be primarily a disease of black people," said Lorna McBarnette, executive deputy commissioner, New York State health department.

—The New York Times

On this day, I

_____ *date*

PATRIOTISM

We are no more aliens to this country or to its institutions than
our brothers in white. We have instituted it; our forefathers paid
dearly for it. . . . Together we planted the tree of liberty and
watered its roots with our tears and blood, and under its
branches we will stay and be sheltered.

—Thomas E. Miller

On this day, I

*date*_____

CHALLENGES

Someone once told me that God figured that I was a pretty good juggler. I could keep a lot of balls in the air at one time. So He said, "Let's see if you can juggle another one."

—*Arthur Ashe*

On this day, I

_____ *date*

STRENGTH

I've talked to so many who believe they are supposed to be
superhuman and bear up under all things. When they don't, they
all too readily look for the fault within themselves.

—*Gloria Naylor*

On this day, I

date _____

ENCOURAGEMENT

You can't regiment spirit, and it is the spirit that counts.
—*Romare Bearden*

On this day, I

_____ *date*

STRUGGLE

We must recognize the awesome demands of time, effort, and
life of serious struggle. The struggle is a long and difficult one;
therefore we must mask no difficulties, tell no lies
and claim no easy victory.

—*Maulana Karenga*

On this day, I

date _____

ACCEPTANCE/
APPRECIATION

I've accepted my reality. I was meant to sound the way I do.

—*Kathleen Battle*

On this day, I

_____ *date*

AFFIRMATIVE ACTION

They have made affirmative action a dirty word.
For us, it's a word that means fairness.

—*Ulysses Jones*

 *On this day, I*

date _____

OPTIMISM

All my life I've had this almost criminal optimism. I didn't care
what happened, the glass was always going to be half full.

—*Quincy Jones*

On this day, I

_____ *date*

IMAGINATION

Nor here, nor there; the roving

fancy flies,

Till some lov'd object strikes her

wandering eyes.

Whose silken fetters all the senses bind,

And soft captivity involves the mind.

—Phillis Wheatley

 On this day, I

date _____

FEAR

Life has frightened me now and then, and if I've ever shown
uncommon bravery, I've failed to notice it.

—*Gordon Parks*

On this day, I

_____ *date*

LOVE

If you're going to be sick and not sure about the future of your
life, it's pretty nice to have someone who loves you.

—*Sammy Davis, Jr.*

On this day, I

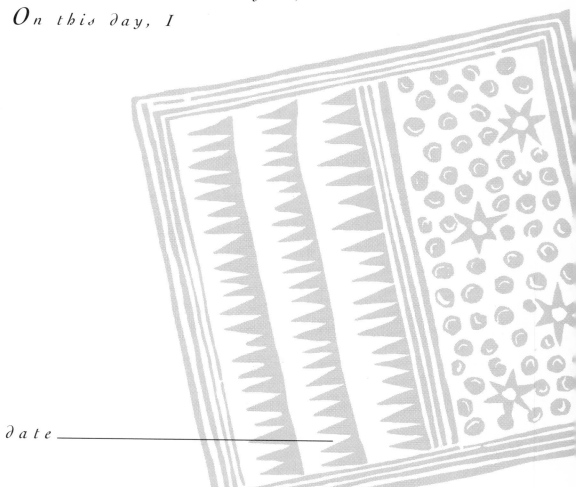

date _____

WINNING

The majority of people in the world don't do what it takes to win. Everyone is looking for the easy road.

—Charles Barkley

O_n this day, I

_____ date

STEREOTYPES

When they approach me they see ... everything
and anything except me.
—*Ralph Ellison, from* The Invisible Man

On this day, I

date _____

ANSWERS/CHOICE

The Met was the first mountain I climbed successfully. I had said no to them when I felt I wasn't ready. When I debuted, I was technically prepared and highly negotiable. I was box-office.

—*Leontyne Price*

On this day, I

date

WANDERING

I was always the chronic wanderer, taking off on a bus or
subway to the end of the line.

—*Cicely Tyson*

On this day, I

date _____

SELF-DELUSION

When face-to-face with one's self . . . there is no cop-out.
—*Edward Kennedy "Duke" Ellington*

On this day, I

_____ *date*

FAITH

Quit talking about dying; if you believe your God is all-
powerful, believe He is powerful enough to
open these prison doors.

—*Ida B. Wells*

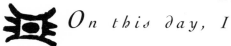 *On this day, I*

date _____

CHILDREN

Black people know how to save our children. Our little children
are the most intuitive, the brightest kids. To reach them
we just have to get back to basics.

—*Nellie Cooke*

On this day, I

_____ *date*

MEDIA IMAGES

The revolution will not be televised.

—Gil Scott Heron

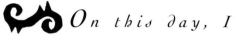 *On this day, I*

date _____

BELIEF

Those who believe in ghosts always see them.
—*Charles V. Roman*

On this day, I

_____ *date*

COURAGE

I became more courageous by doing the very things I needed to be courageous for—first, a little, and badly. Then, bit by bit, more and better. Being avidly—sometimes annoyingly—curious and persistent about discovering how others were doing what I wanted to do.

—Audre Lorde

On this day, I

date _____

COMPASSION

Judge not the brother! There are secrets in his heart
that you might weep to see.

—*Egbert Martin*

On this day, I

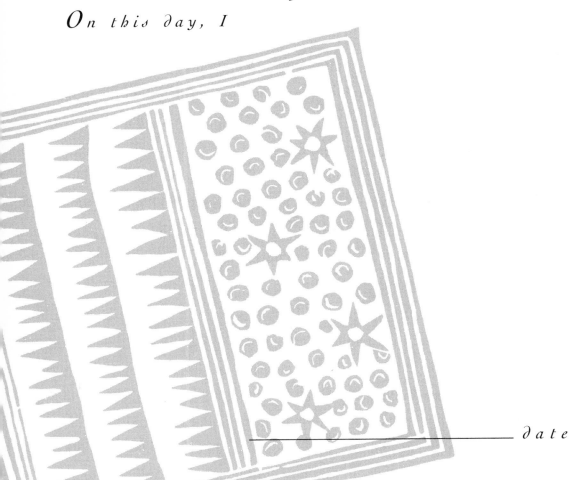

_____ *date*

STRENGTH

They'll never count me among the broken men.

—*George Lester Johnson*

On this day, I

date _____

QUESTIONING

O my body, make of me always a man who questions.

—*Frantz Fanon*

*O*n this day, I

_____ *date*

ACTIVISM

If you have a microphone, you have a responsibility
to make your opinions known.

—*John Singleton*

On this day, I

date _____

POWER

Power concedes nothing without demand;
it never has and it never will.
—*Frederick Douglass*

On this day, I

_____ *date*

SILENCE

If you're silent for a long time, people just arrive in your mind.

—*Alice Walker*

On this day, I

date _____

ENVIRONMENTALISM

Treat the world well. . . . It was not given to you by your parents. . . . It was lent to you by your children.

—*Kenyan proverb*

On this day, I

_____ *date*

PRIDE

I haunted the city dumps and the trash piles behind hotels, retrieving discarded linen and kitchenware . . . broken chairs. . . . Everything was scoured and mended. This was part of the training to salvage, to reconstruct, to make bricks without straw.

—*Mary McLeod Bethune*

 On this day, I

date _____

SEX

A woman's love is a [man's] privilege and not his right.
—*Terry McMillan, from* Waiting to Exhale

On this day, I

_____ *date*

HOME

Don't you realize that the sea is the home of the water? All water is off on a journey unlessen it's in the sea, and it's homesick, and bound to make its way home someday.

—*Zora Neale Hurston, from* Seraph on the Suwanee

On this day, I

*date*_____

CHANGE

Each time I sing, it's a new experience for me. None of the roles
I have done has yet reached a pinnacle: They are always
evolving and being reevaluated.

—*Kathleen Battle*

 *On this day, I*

_____ *date*

UNFAIRNESS/CHALLENGES

She informed us regularly and matter-of-factly that we had to be twice as good as white children in everything we attempted in life. "That way you got half a chance of making it."

—*Bebe Moore Campbell, from* Sweet Summer

On this day, I

date _____

FULFILLMENT

The human heart is a strange mystery.

—*Alexandre Dumas, fils*

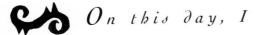 *On this day, I*

_____ *date*

PATRIOTISM

I feel that I am a citizen of the American dream, that the revolutionary struggle of which I am a part is a struggle against the American nightmare.

—*Eldridge Cleaver*

On this day, I

date _____

ADVERSITY

In every adversity, look for the benefit that can come out of it.
Even bad experiences offer benefits; but you
have to look for them.

—*John E. Copage*

On this day, I

_____ *date*

POWER

Successful black men seem instinctively to understand something of the nature of power — that while it may be denied, it can also be assumed, claimed, seized, and exercised, for it is neither finite nor ordained.

—*Audrey Edwards and Craig K. Polite, from* Children of the Dream

On this day, I

date _____

UNIQUENESS

For a long time, I thought I was ugly and disfigured. This made me shy and timid, and I often reacted to insults that were not intended. . . . I believe, though, that it was from this period . . . that I really began to see people and things.

—*Alice Walker*

On this day, I

_____*date*

APPRECIATION

I'll pick up little books or cards and send them to [my son] with
a message that may simply say, "You're a wonderful son."
—*Natalie Cole*

On this day, I

date _____

ACTION

When the snake is in the house, one need not
discuss the matter at length.

—Ewe proverb

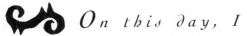 *On this day, I*

_____ *date*

FAITH

My relationship with God has helped me avoid problems others have run into.

—*Barry Sanders*

On this day, I

date _____

SUPPORT

I could draw a circle on a piece of paper and my
mother made me feel like Van Gogh.

—*Damon Wayans*

On this day, I

_____ *date*

POWER

Power doesn't mean you're acting like a man, or you're a bully or a bitch. It's that you don't let people step on you.

—*Sharon Monplaisir*

On this day, I

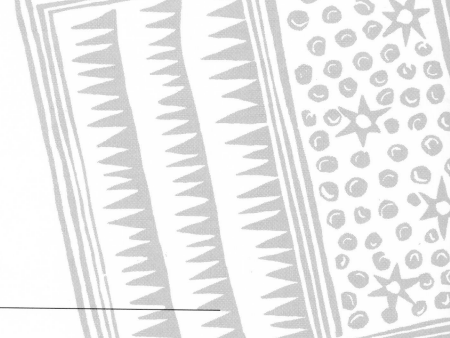

*date*_____

AGE

There ain't nothin' an ol' man can do but bring
me a message from a young one.

—*Jackie "Moms" Mabley, in one of her comic routines*

On this day, I

_____ *date*

INDEPENDENCE

People thought they had to protect me from a lot of things. In doing so, they denied me a chance to grow, to experience the things that give a person a certain amount of growth and maturity. I've had to make up for all that lost time in recent years, but I don't blame anyone.

—*Kareem Abdul-Jabbar*

On this day, I

date _____

COLLECTIVE WORK/ COLLECTIVE RESPONSIBILITY

Injustice doesn't have to occur to me personally, but I react personally and I am compelled to do something about it.

—*Rose Sanders*

On this day, I

_____ *date*

PERSEVERANCE/WILL

Life is like a slot machine. The coins you put into it are work
and ideas. And, unlike a Las Vegas slot machine, you can
influence the chances of winning with your will.

—*Bessie Copage*

On this day, I

date _____

SELF-LOVE

Long tresses down to the floor can be beautiful, if you
have that, but learn to love what you have.

—*Anita Baker*

On this day, I

_____ *date*

WISDOM

At twenty-two, I thought I knew everything. Now, at sixty-seven, I find I haven't tasted a drop from the sea of knowledge. The more I learn, the more I find out how little I know.

—*John E. Copage*

 On this day, I

date _____

FIGHTING

I got into very few fights when I played for the Celtics, but every single one of them was in the last quarter, after the game was decided. You have to choose when to fight.

—*Bill Russell*

On this day, I

_____ *date*

RESILIENCY

I still dream big at times, but when my dreams pull apart, as they sometimes do, I don't press the panic button.

—Gordon Parks

On this day, I

date _____

HOPE

We never lost hope despite the segregated world of this rural
town because we had adults who gave us a sense of a
future—and black folk had an extra lot of problems, and we
were taught that we could struggle and change them.

—Marian Wright Edelman

On this day, I

_____ *date*

READING/EDUCATION

If I was not reading in the [prison] library, I was reading on my bunk. You couldn't have gotten me out of books with a wedge.

—*Malcolm X*

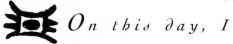 *On this day, I*

date _____

GUILT

Not much is going to come from another guilt
trip for white America.

—*Wyatt Tee Walker*

On this day, I

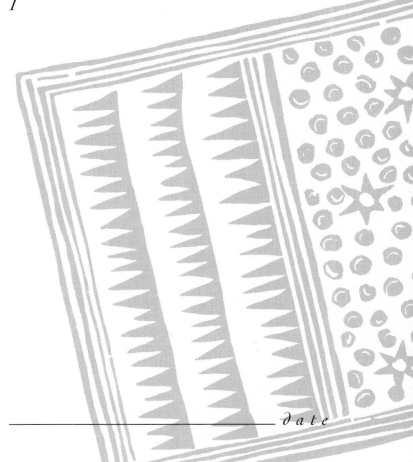

date

DIGNITY

No race can prosper till it learns that there is as much dignity
in tilling a field as in writing a poem.

—*Booker T. Washington*

On this day, I

date _____

Appropriateness

Eating when you are hungry and sleeping when you are sleepy.
That is the ultimate wisdom.

—*Bessie Copage*

 On this day, I

_____ *date*

ASSISTANCE

My mind is overtaxed. Brave and courageous as I am, I feel that creeping on of that inevitable thing, a breakdown, if I cannot get some immediate relief. I need somebody to come and get me.

—*Mary McLeod Bethune*

 On this day, I

*date*_____

TOLERANCE

A person is a person because he recognizes others as persons.
—*Desmond Tutu*

On this day, I

_____ *date*

APPEARANCE

Peop le should start dressing for success before
they're successful—not after!
—*Willi Smith*

On this day, I

date _____

CHILDREN

We think that our children are ours, but they are only our seed.
Their reason and purpose has something to do with them, and I
don't think we can take credit for that or try to control it.

—*Don Cherry*

On this day, I

_____ *date*

JEALOUSY

Rivalry is better than envy.

—Mongo proverb

On this day, I

date _____

RESPONSIBILITY

It is quite easy to shout slogans, to sign manifestos, but it is quite a different matter to build, manage, command, spend days and nights seeking the solution of problems.

—*Patrice Lumumba*

On this day, I

_____ *date*

ACCEPTANCE

The only thing you have to be that's important in life . . . is just
go on being your own normal, black, beautiful selves
as women, as human beings.

—*Fannie Lou Hamer*

 *On this day, I*

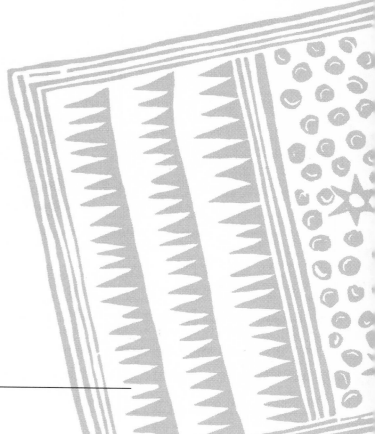

date _____

CONFIDENCE

My mother convinced me to learn to enjoy having people tell
me I can't do something. Now it's second nature;
I love to prove people wrong.

—*Andre Ware*

On this day, I

_____ *date*

EXCELLENCE

Whatever you do, do with all your might.

—*Aesop, from "The Boy and the Nettles"*

On this day, I

date _____

FRESH STARTS

Facing the rising sun of our new day begun, Let us
march on till victory is won.

—*James Weldon Johnson*

On this day, I

_____ *date*

ENTHUSIASM

If a man is called to be a street sweeper, he should sweep streets
even as Michelangelo painted or Beethoven composed music
or Shakespeare wrote poetry.

—*Martin Luther King, Jr.*

On this day, I

*date*_____

MOTIVATION

It's been said that no one can really motivate anyone else; all you can do is instill a positive attitude and hope it catches on.

—*Eddie Robinson*

 On this day, I

_____ *date*

SELF-DISCOVERY

There is a complexity about human life that this society does not supply. From the time you're born it makes you decide what you're going to be and where you're going to stand and are you this or are you that.

—*Bernice Johnson Reagon*

On this day, I

date _____

PRIVATE THOUGHTS

Blessed is the man who to himself has kept

The high creations of his soul;

Who from his friends as from the grave,
Expected nothing of esteem!

—*Aleksandr Sergeyevich Pushkin*

On this day, I

_____ *date*

RISK

So many people are afraid of taking even the smallest chance.
They cling to dull routines as if those routines are life rafts.

—*Overheard at Junior's restaurant in Brooklyn*

On this day, I

*date*_____

PREPARATION

If you're going to play the game properly, you'd
better know every rule.

—*Barbara Jordan*

On this day, I

_____ *date*

OBLIGATIONS

I am still learning—how to take joy in all the people I am, how to use all my selves in the service of what I believe, how to accept when I fail and rejoice when I succeed.

—Audre Lorde

On this day, I

date _____

RECEPTIVITY

It is hard to talk about yourself all day. . . . You learn when you're with other ideas, other books, other friends. Talking about yourself can't advance your life.

—*Yannick Noah*

On this day, I

date

COURAGE

I am old enough to know that victory is often a thing deferred, and rarely at the summit of courage. . . . What is at the summit of courage, I think, is freedom. The freedom that comes with the knowledge that no earthly thing can break you.

—*Paula Giddings*

On this day, I

date _____

GENERALIZING

I trust women. I was raised by women, by my godmother,
my grandmother and my mother. . . . I understand
women. I know women.

—*Arsenio Hall*

On this day, I

_____ *date*

ART

Art is the material evidence that reminds us of the wealth
of our culture—of who we are.

—*Mary Schmidt Campbell*

On this day, I

date _____

CHOICES

Before me there were no actors in my family and no convicts.

—*Charles Dutton, who turned his life around after
spending more than seven years in prison*

On this day, I

_____ *date*

MISTAKES

There is a way to look at the past. Don't hide from it.
It will not catch you if you don't repeat it.

—*Pearl Bailey*

On this day, I

*date*_____

VALUES

Work must be inspired by the right ideals, and education must not simply teach work, but life based on those ideals.
— *W.E.B. Du Bois*

On this day, I

_____ *date*

FRIENDSHIP

An enemy slaughters, a friend distributes.

—Fulfulde proverb

On this day, I

date _____

HASTE

Before shooting, one must aim.

—*Nigerian proverb*

On this day, I

_____*date*

BALANCE

I was the best . . . and it was a drag. Now I just want to be good, and stay good.

—*Eddie Murphy*

On this day, I

date _____

MENTAL AND PHYSICAL HEALTH

The head and the body must serve each other.

—From a Wolof folktale

On this day, I

_____ *date*

STRUGGLE

People don't understand the kind of fight it takes to record what you want to record the way you want to record it.

—Billie Holiday

On this day, I

date _____

PROGRESS

We ask not that others bear our burden, but do not obstruct
our pathway, and we will throw off our burdens as we run.

—*Reverdy Ransom*

On this day, I

_____ *date*

VISUALIZATION

Some people are your relatives but others are your ancestors,
and you choose the ones you want to have as ancestors.
You create yourself out of those values.

—Ralph Ellison

On this day, I

date _____

THINKING SMART

The issue is no longer where you sit on the bus or whether you
can drive it; it's whether you can develop the capital
to own the bus company.

—*William H. Gray III*

 On this day, I

_____ *date*

LOOKING BACK

Don't look back. Something might be gaining on you.

—*Leroy "Satchel" Paige*

On this day, I

date _____

CYCLES

By going and coming, a bird weaves its nest.

—*Ashanti proverb, West Africa*

On this day, I

_____ *date*

SELF-RESPECT

One cannot give to a person that which he already possesses.

—Toussaint L'Ouverture, Proclamation, March 1, 1802

On this day, I

*date*_____

POSITIVE THOUGHTS

If I walked a perfect line, there'd be people who said I was too
perfect. . . . There will always be naysayers, but I
won't give them free rent in my head.

—Carl Lewis

On this day, I

_____ *date*

REVENGE

It is Martin King who taught that a real moral struggle
seeks to win partners, not to leave victims.

—*Maulana Karenga*

On this day, I

date _____

WORRY

Many people worry, but they don't do anything about it.
—*Pearl Bailey*

On this day, I

_____ *date*

PRIDE

Don't be ashamed to show your colors, and to own them.
— *William Wells Brown*

On this day, I

date _____

SUCCESS

You can't hurry up good times by waitin' for 'em.

—U.S. proverb

On this day, I

_____ *date*

PARENTS

I cannot forget my mother. Though not as sturdy as others, she
is my bridge. When I needed to get across, she steadied herself
long enough for me to run across safely.

—*Renita Weems*

On this day, I

*date*_____

VISIBILITY

You've got to find a way to make people know you're there.

—*Nikki Giovanni*

On this day, I

_____ *date*

FLEXIBILITY AND ACHIEVEMENT

Necessity has no law.

—*Terence, from* The Eunuch, *Act V*

On this day, I

date _____

PERSEVERANCE

Ev'ry day fishin' day, but no ev'ry day catch fish.
—*Bahamian proverb*

On this day, I

_____ *date*

SELF-PITY

But before my thoughts led me further in the direction of self-pity, I brought them to a halt, reminding myself that this was precisely what solitary confinement was supposed to evoke.

—*Angela Davis*

On this day, I

date _____

HUMOR

If you don't have a sense of humor, you become a scowling time bomb, striking out at people who are dear to you.

—*Ishmael Reed*

On this day, I

_____ *date*

MOMENTUM

The sight of freedom looming on the horizon should
encourage us to redouble our efforts.

—*Nelson Mandela*

On this day, I

*date*_____

BLACK PRIDE

Racism should make us [African-Americans] love one another,
not disrespect or murder each other.

—*James Goodwin*

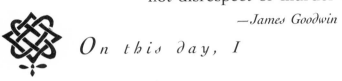 *On this day, I*

_____*date*

EXCELLENCE

Show me someone content with mediocrity and I'll show
you someone destined for failure.

—*Johnetta Cole*

On this day, I

date _____

MOODINESS

Yes, I can be moody. I can be bitchy. . . . But when I'm moody
and bitchy, I keep my butt at home.

—*Anita Baker*

On this day, I

_____*date*

SEX

Heaven and earth! How is it that bodies join but never meet?

—*Beah Richards*

On this day, I

date _____

DIRECTION

The way she wastes her time, the way she drifts through the
office, you feel that all she wants to do with her life
is to lose it somewhere.

—*Black executive about one of his employees*

On this day, I

_____ *date*

PROGRESS

We must not, in trying to think about how we can make a big difference, ignore the small daily differences we can make which, over time, add up to big differences that we often cannot foresee.

—*Marian Wright Edelman*

On this day, I

date _____

INSPIRATION

As I grow older, part of my emotional survival plan must
be to actively seek inspiration instead of passively
waiting for it to find me.

—*Bebe Moore Campbell*

On this day, I

_____ *date*

SELF-DETERMINATION

I don't see why we can't be good in one thing and try to
experiment in being good at another.
—*Naomi Campbell*

On this day, I

date _____

APPROPRIATENESS

When the music changes, so does the dance.

—*Hausa proverb*

On this day, I

_____ *date*

CHANGE

Life is like an enormous darkened room in which somebody
keeps moving the furniture; you can't tell from moment to
moment whether you're about to plop into your favorite
easy chair or a potted cactus.

—*Eric V. Copage*

On this day, I

date _____

CENSORING OURSELVES

A lot of times we censor ourselves before
the censor even gets there.

—*Spike Lee*

On this day, I

date

EXCELLENCE

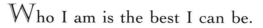

Who I am is the best I can be.

—*Leontyne Price*

On this day, I

date _____

SELF-WORTH

The price of your hat isn't the measure of your brain.

—African-American proverb

On this day, I

_____ *date*

POWER

You can either try to get inside and have some influence, or you can stay outside and be pure and powerless.

—*James Brown*

On this day, I

date _____

SELFISHNESS

Sometimes you give so much that it hurts. You give and give and give, and you have nothing that belongs to you. It's important to have something that belongs to you . . . something inside you, to keep to yourself.

—*Yannick Noah*

On this day, I

date

FLEXIBILITY/PURPOSE

By any means necessary.
—*Malcolm X*

On this day, I

date _____

HERITAGE

The fruit must have a stem before it grows.

—*Jabo proverb, Liberia*

On this day, I

_____ *date*

MODESTY

Let's not get too full of ourselves. Let's leave space for God to come into the room.

—*Quincy Jones*

On this day, I

date _____

KINDNESS

My father, as an adult, did not go to church, but he was
kinder than swarms of church-goers.

—*Gwendolyn Brooks*

On this day, I

_____ *date*

UNITY

There is no separate freedom or dignity for
African men and women.

—*Maulana Karenga*

On this day, I

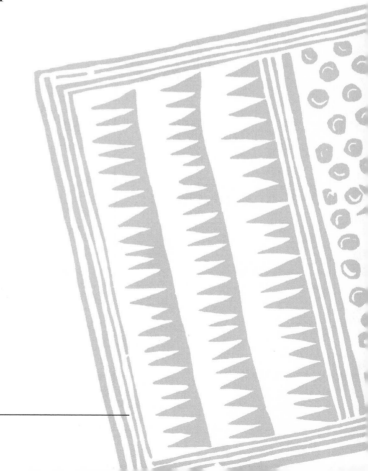

date _____

VISION

·····························

I had to practically hypnotize myself into thinking
I was going to be a success.

—*John Singleton*

On this day, I

_____ *date*

BLACKNESS

Don't say I don't have soul or what you consider to be
"Blackness." I know what my color is.
—*Whitney Houston*

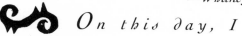 *On this day, I*

*date*_____

DISCRETION

The discreet man knows how to hold his tongue.
—*Malagasy proverb*

On this day, I

_____ *date*

CHALLENGES

Go all the way to the edge, don't settle for a safe position.

—Cordell Reagon

On this day, I

*date*_____

SELF-DETERMINATION

Stand on your own two Black feet and fight like hell
for your place in the world. . . .
—*Amy Jacques Garvey*

On this day, I

_____ *date*

NUTRITION

The empty bag cannot stand up.
—*Haitian proverb*

On this day, I

*date*_____

WHITE PEOPLE

I believe there are some sincere white people.
But I think they should prove it.

—*Malcolm X*

On this day, I

_____ *date*

DEPRESSION

Most people who are depressed have a legitimate reason to be. There's a healthy part of your ego that tells you something's not right. The problem with depression is that it can become generalized to encompass your entire existence.

—*Craig K. Polite*

On this day, I

date _____

APPRECIATION

The one being carried does not realize how
far away the town is.
—*Nigerian proverb*

On this day, I

_____*date*

SELF-LOVE

I have always lived well, bought fresh flowers
and eaten filet mignon.
—*Terry McMillan*

On this day, I

date _____

ORIGINALITY

When I was doing my talk show in Baltimore, I used to watch
Donahue to figure out how to do it. That's the truth. I stopped
... because I found myself saying, "Is the caller there?" —
and repeating things just the way he did.

—*Oprah Winfrey*

On this day, I

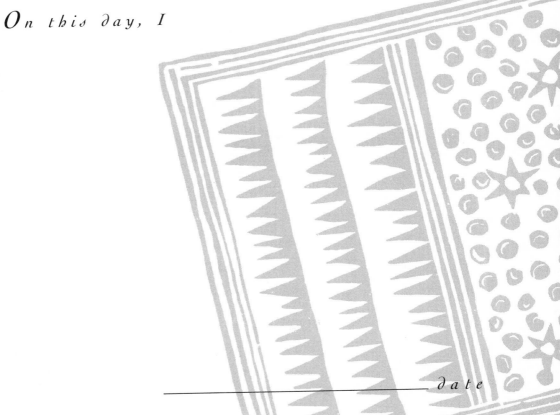

_____ *date*

TRADITION

The young cannot teach tradition to the old.

—Yoruba proverb

On this day, I

date _____

CRITICISM

Before healing others, heal thyself.
— *Wolof proverb*

On this day, I

_____ *date*

OPTIMISM

My idea of life is to forget the bad and live for the
good there is in it. This is my motto.

—*Squire Dowd*

On this day, I

date _____

WORK

*I go fur adgitatin'. But I believe dere is works
belongs wid adgitatin', too.*

—*Sojourner Truth*

On this day, I

_____ date

GRIEF

A month after her death, I found the courage to sleep in
Mama's bed. I wanted to feel her spirit, even prayed, insane
woman that I had become, for an apparition or a
voice. . . . I felt nothing except pain.

—*Gloria Wade-Gayles*

On this day, I

*date*_____

EMOTION

Emotion is what makes me what I am today.
It makes me play bigger than I am.
—*Charles Barkley*

On this day, I

_____ *date*

PERSUASIVENESS

If there's one thing I know, it's how to sell the show.
—*Muhammad Ali*

On this day, I

date _____

OPTIMISM

It's easy 'nough to titter w'en de stew is
smokin' hot,
But hit's mighty ha'd to giggle
w'en de's nuffin' in de pot.

—*Paul Laurence Dunbar, from "Philosophy"*

On this day, I

_____ *date*

RELATIONSHIPS

Never follow a beast into its lair.

—*Chuana proverb*

On this day, I

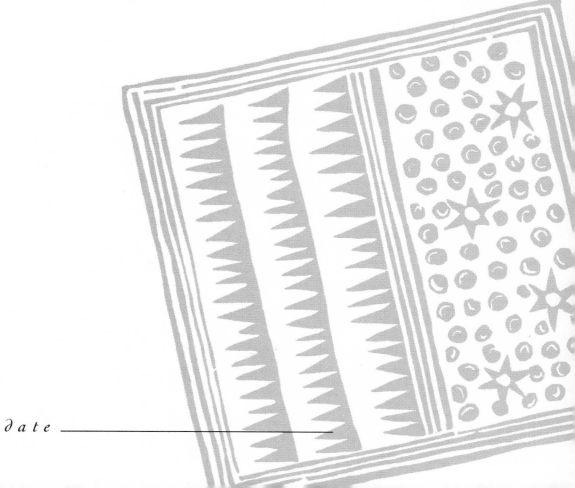

date _____

RELAXATION

The most important part of good health and relief from stress is surrounding yourself with people who love you.

—*Wilma Rudolph*

On this day, I

_____ *date*

WILL/COURAGE

Behind each act of courage you will find an unbreakable will.

—*Overheard in a Detroit office*

On this day, I

date _____

NATIONALISM

The nationalist space is a womb space, where you can be
nurtured in a positive way. But you don't live in a womb.
Babies who aren't born, die.

—*Bernice Johnson Reagon*

On this day, I

date

PREPAREDNESS/ RECEPTIVITY

Before eating, open thy mouth.
— *Wolof proverb*

On this day, I

date _____

WORK

I learned that no matter what you may or may not have, as perceived by a misguided community about what is valuable, people understand hard work and talent—and it can prevail.

—*Maxine Waters*

On this day, I

_____ *date*

SELF-MOTIVATION

I came out of the sixties, when people had commitment and passion, and when there was aliveness and purpose.

—*Barbara Ann Teer*

On this day, I

date _____

HURRYING

Haste has no blessing.
—*Swahili proverb*

On this day, I

_____ *date*

THINKING

Nothing pains some people more than having to think.

—*Martin Luther King, Jr.*

 *On this day, I*

date _____

WISDOM

Wisdom is greater than knowledge, for wisdom includes knowledge and the due use of it.

—*Joseph Sevelli Capponi*

On this day, I

_____ *date*

SELF-DETERMINATION

If I didn't define myself for myself, I would be crunched into
other people's fantasies for me and eaten alive.

—*Audre Lorde*

On this day, I

date _____

HERITAGE

What all achieving blacks successfully do is turn the color of
black into the color of victory.

—*Audrey Edwards and Craig K. Polite, from* Children of the Dream

On this day, I

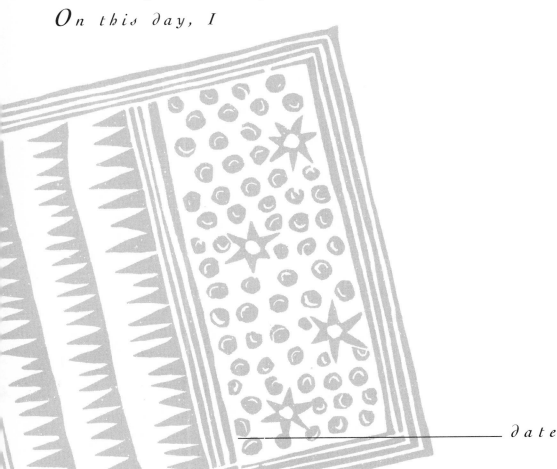

_____ *date*

ABILITY

Before we were allowed to play basketball, we were told we
didn't have the ability. Before we were allowed to box,
we were told we didn't have the ability.

—*Eric V. Copage*

On this day, I

date _____

FLEXIBILITY

Always have more than one iron in the fire.

—Common saying overheard in a New York City office

On this day, I

_____ *date*

PLAY

I do work very hard, and when I finish a project, I can party all
night. Or I can be happy going somewhere very quiet with
my kids and digging holes in the sand.

—Debbie Allen

On this day, I

date _____

PRIVACY

There comes a point when you really have to spend time with
yourself to know who you are. Black people need
to be with ourselves.

—*Bernice Johnson Reagon*

On this day, I

_____ *date*

DREAMS

It's time to move from hope to making what we hoped about
and dreamed about real. Now is the time for the
prophecy to be fulfilled.

—*Calvin O. Butts*

On this day, I

date _____

INDIVIDUALITY

"Young ladies don't wear shorts when they go down the road."
Grandma uttered this gravely, without the least hint of a smile.

—*Bebe Moore Campbell, from* Sweet Summer

On this day, I

_____ *date*

SAVORING

Exhaust the little moment.
—*Gwendolyn Brooks*

On this day, I

date _____

ORIGINALITY

In search of my mother's garden, I found my own.
—*Alice Walker*

On this day, I

_____ *date*

AUTHENTICITY

The varieties of human choice and thought are not very
willingly accepted when the subject is Afro-Americans.

—*Stanley Crouch*

On this day, I

date _____

PARENTHOOD

I had ... found that motherhood was a profession by itself,
just like schoolteaching and lecturing.
—*Ida B. Wells*

On this day, I

_____ *date*

PATRIOTISM

The fact is that blacks are not outside the American mainstream
but, in [Ralph] Ellison's words, have always been
"one of its major tributaries."

—*Claude M. Steele*

On this day, I

date _____

SUCCESS

If you can somehow think and dream of success in small steps,
every time you make a step, every time you accomplish a small
goal, it gives you confidence to go on from there.

—John H. Johnson

On this day, I

_____ *date*

SELF-PRAISE

You have to know that your real home is within.
—*Quincy Jones*

On this day, I

date _____

COLLECTIVE RESPONSIBILITY

We do not live for ourselves only, but for our wives and children, who are as dear to us as those of any other men.

—*Abraham*

On this day, I

_____ date

SKILLS

I don't believe that you have to be mean to be successful in the
ring. I don't understand why some boxers are motivated by hate.
The way I see it, it's possible to be a good boxer and
a good person at the same time.

—*Evander Holyfield*

On this day, I

∂ a t e _____

MIND POWER

There is a way to provide against the onslaught of poverty. It is the recognition of the power of the mind.

—*A. G. Gaston*

On this day, I

_____ *date*

ROLE MODELS

Teddy [Roosevelt] was very close to me because we both had asthma and would stay awake at night with our back propped up by a pillow. But he overcame it, went to Harvard and became a great speaker. So I decided I had to go to Harvard, too, although at eight I didn't know exactly what it was.

—*Cornell West*

On this day, I

*date*_____

PERSEVERANCE

Black people told me, "Yo, baby, you're black. This is America, still the white man's country. Forget it."

—*Arsenio Hall*

On this day, I

_____ *date*

PATIENCE

Every dog has his day; there is a time for all things.

—*Terence, from* The Eunuch

On this day, I

date _____

SUBSTANCE

I'm not a star, I'm a writer. I don't want to be a star.
—*Terry McMillan*

On this day, I

_____ *date*

SELFISHNESS

It is time for every one of us to roll up our sleeves and put
ourselves at the top of our commitment list.

—*Marian Wright Edelman*

On this day, I

date _____

CRISES

In every crisis there is a message. Crises are nature's way of forcing change—breaking down old structures, shaking loose negative habits so that something new and better can take their place.

—*Susan Taylor*

 On this day, I

_____ *date*

AFRICAN-AMERICANS

I thought that this beautiful feeling I'd shared with my immediate family was exclusive to them. I saw instead that the black feeling — the warmth, the love, the laughter, the spontaneity — extended beyond my household.

—*Janet Jackson*

On this day, I

date _____

SILENCE

Silence is also speech.

—Fulfulde proverb

On this day, I

_____ *date*

PRIDE

I'm perfectly satisfied to be an American Negro,
tough as it all is.

—*Jessie Fauset*

On this day, I

date _____

MUSIC

There is no such thing that all blacks have rhythm. It's not that they're born with rhythm, but in black homes you always hear music. It becomes instinctive, a lot rubs off.

—*Arthur Mitchell*

On this day, I

_____ *date*

HOPE

Hope is the pillar of the world.

—*Kanuri proverb*

On this day, I

date _____

PRIDE

Aunt Jemima is the black woman who cooked and cleaned, struggled, brought up her own family and a white family. And if I'm ashamed of Aunt Jemima—her head rag, her hips, her color—then I'm ashamed of my people.

—*Maxine Waters*

On this day, I

_____ *date*

AFFIRMATION

I am/I can.

—Graffito in Harlem

On this day, I

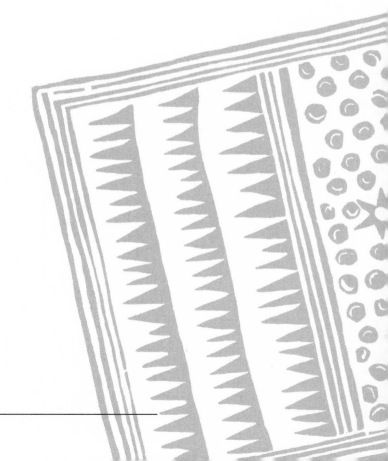

date

CONFIDENCE

If I can make you think I'm King Kong, I've won the match.
—*Lynette Love, Tae Kwon Do Olympic Gold Medalist*

On this day, I

_____ *date*

ORIGINALITY

I decided, if I'm going to be poor and black and all, the least
thing I'm going to do is try and find out who I am.
I created everything about me.

—*Ornette Coleman*

On this day, I

date _____

FEELING

Man, if you gotta ask, you'll never know.
—*Louis Armstrong, on the definition of jazz*

On this day, I

_____*date*

ACCEPTANCE

*S*tart with what you know and build on what you have.

—*Kwame Nkrumah*

*O*n *this day, I*

date _____

FULFILLMENT

I find, in being black, a thing of beauty: a joy;
a strength; a secret cup of gladness.

—*Ossie Davis, from* Purlie Victorious

On this day, I

_____ *date*

V ANITY

V anity is the beginning of corruption.

—*Joaquim Maria Machado de Assis*

On this day, I

date _____

DESPAIR

After distress, solace.
—*Swahili proverb*

On this day, I

_____ *date*

GRACEFULNESS

My whole *nation* is graceful. Nobody has to tell us how to walk
or how to stand. We have an air, a dignity: Whatever
happens, you keep your head up.

—*Iman*

On this day, I

date _____

FULFILLMENT

I don't think there's anything in the world I can't do. . . . In my creative source, whatever that is, I don't see why I can't sculpt. Why shouldn't I? Human beings sculpt. I'm a human being.

—*Maya Angelou*

On this day, I

_____ *date*

CHALLENGES

She was very stern and very firm. She pushed me, and I didn't like it for a long time. But now I push myself, because I know that my limits are more than I thought they were.

—*Yasmeen Graham*

On this day, I

date _____

LOOKING BACK

The underdog does not stop to philosophize about his position.
—*Paul Laurence Dunbar, from* The Fanatics

On this day, I

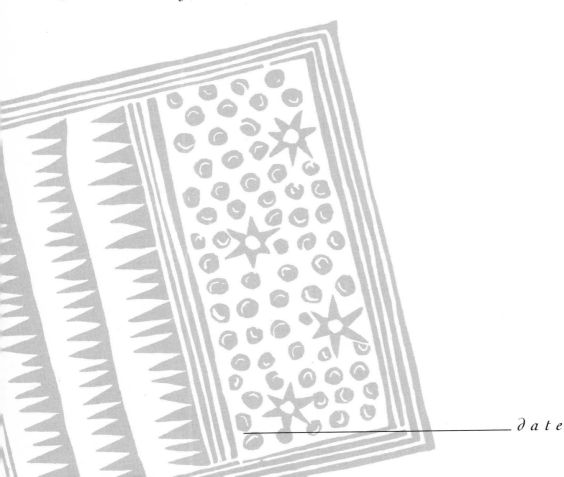

_____ *date*

SELF-HELP

Solve your own problem by curing your own defects.

—*Joseph Sevelli Capponi*

On this day, I

date _____

BIGOTRY

I grew up hearing about the ways black people were abused, but we were also told we were much better in many ways than the people who were doing this. We just absolutely did not understand why white people had to be so contrary.

—*Bernice Johnson Reagon*

On this day, I

_____ *date*

COMPASSION

Make some muscle in your head,
but use the muscle in your heart.

—*Imamu Amiri Baraka*

On this day, I

date _____

ACCOMPLISHMENT

You can't hang around bathing your body in the
reflection of a trophy.

—*Bill Cosby*

On this day, I

_____ *date*

ADVISERS

I have wise advisers . . . and I ask them, "Are my goals realistic? Am I moving in a good direction?" Even though I'm the one who finally decides . . . I require a wide range of opinion.

—*Janet Jackson*

On this day, I

date _____

LOVE

Love is mutually feeding each other, not one
living on another like a ghoul.
—*Bessie Head*

 On this day, I

_____ *date*

ACCOMPLISHMENT

People will know you're serious when you produce.

—*Muhammad Ali*

On this day, I

date _____

BEGINNINGS

A forest that has sheltered you, you should not
call a patch of scrub.

—Oji proverb

On this day, I

_____ *date*

INTIMIDATION

I've never learned to be afraid of people who are
more powerful than I.

—*Jamaica Kincaid*

On this day, I

*date*_____

VICTIMHOOD

One of the recurring success themes in the African-American community is the frequency with which being a victim actually drives ambition.

—*Audrey Edwards and Craig K. Polite, from* Children of the Dream

On this day, I

_____ *date*

HUMOR

Funny is an attitude.
—*Flip Wilson*

On this day, I

date _____

SELF-ESTEEM

If you are not feeling good about you, what you're wearing
outside doesn't mean a thing.

—*Leontyne Price*

On this day, I

_____ *date*

SELF-HELP

If the white man gives you anything, just remember, when he
gets ready he will take it right back.

—Fannie Lou Hamer

On this day, I

date _____

INNER PEACE

My life is actually better than it appears because of my inner peace. I used to be my own worst enemy. But that has changed.

—*Oprah Winfrey*

On this day, I

_____ *date*

FAMILY

My family has always given me a place to be,
a place to be loved in and to love.

—*Billy Dee Williams*

On this day, I

date _____

UNITY

....

I am because we are; and since we are, therefore I am.

—*John Mbuti*

On this day, I

_____ *date*

SELF-DETERMINATION

There are people who say I'm crazy. That's okay.
I can live with that.

—*Carl Lewis*

On this day, I

date _____

COLLECTIVE WORK AND RESPONSIBILITY

No matter what accomplishment you make,
somebody helps you.

—*Althea Gibson*

On this day, I

_____ *date*

COOPERATIVE ECONOMICS

My father was the kind who would say, "If a black
man opens a store, go shop in it."
—*Calvin O. Butts*

On this day, I

date _____

PURPOSE

On the way to one's beloved, there are no hills.
—*Kenyan proverb*

On this day, I

date

CREATIVITY

I know why the caged bird sings!

—*Paul Laurence Dunbar*

On this day, I

date _____

PERMISSIONS

ABOUT THE AUTHOR

Eric V. Copage has contributed articles to the pages of *The New York Times Magazine,* where he is currently an editor. He was a staff reporter for *Life* magazine and the New York *Daily News* and a music columnist for *Essence* magazine. He has a degree in ethnomusicology and has traveled extensively in West Africa. He is also the author of *Kwanzaa: An African-American Celebration of Culture and Cooking* (William Morrow, 1991) and *Black Pearls for Parents* (Quill/William Morrow, 1995).

ABOUT THE COVER

The illustration is adapted by artist Debra Morton Hoyt from a detail on a piece of African fabric. The strong, tall flowers represent individual strength; the soaring bird represents pride; the water implies reflection; and the sunrise is a symbol of inspiration.